CHAPTERS IN HISTORY

Who Conducted the Underground Railroad?

And Other Questions About the Path to Freedom

by Peter and Connie Roop

SCHOLASTIC

For all of the Olivers, especially Anita
and our guardian angel Clarence!

—C. R. and P. R.

ISBN-13: 978-0-439-02524-9
ISBN-10: 0-439-02524-9

Text copyright © 2008 by Peter and Connie Roop
Illustrations copyright © 2008 by Scholastic Inc.

12 11 10 9 8   11 12 13/0

Printed in the U.S.A.
First printing, February 2008

Contents

CHAPTER 1

Did the Underground Railroad Really Run Underground?

No. The Underground Railroad didn't run underground. It wasn't even a real railroad! The Underground Railroad was a secret pathway from slavery in the South to freedom in the North. Between 1810 and 1850 over 100,000 African-American slaves traveled on the Underground Railroad to northern states and Canada where they could be free. They were helped by many brave people along the way.

Life as a Slave

Life was very hard for slaves. They did what their owners ordered them to do. They worked from sunrise to sunset. Some worked in fields. Some worked in their owners' homes. Slave children began working when they were only six years old.

No matter what jobs the slaves did they were not free to live their own lives. Slaves were punished when they did not do what they were ordered to do. Many slaves dreamed about escaping to freedom. But they would need help.

Help on the Road to Freedom

African-American slaves fleeing to freedom had people help them along the way. Sometimes it might be another slave who gave the runaway slave food or a place to sleep. Many white people who did not believe in slavery helped, too. They gave clothes, food, money, medicine, and shelter to runaway slaves. Many free African-Americans helped slaves escape to freedom, as well. These helpers showed the runaway slaves the best places to hide. They showed them the best routes heading north. They gave the slaves money to help them escape on the Underground Railroad.

The Underground Railroad

People used railroad words to talk about the escaping slaves. Runaway slaves were called "passengers," "packages," and "cargo." The people helping them were known as "conductors." Places where runaway slaves could be safe were called "stations." The trails the slaves took were called "routes." Before long, people called this secret network of escaping slaves and their helpers "The Underground Railroad."

FACT

Another name for the safe resting places was "depots."

The Underground Railroad Gets Its Name

No one knows who named the Underground Railroad. One story says it happened this way. . . .

Slave catchers chased some runaway slaves into Pennsylvania. Suddenly, the escaping slaves disappeared! The slave catchers looked and looked but could not find the runaway slaves anywhere. One puzzled slave catcher said, "There must be an underground railroad somewhere!"

From then on the Underground Railroad was rolling!

Running Away to Freedom

Slaves had to be brave to run away. Some spent weeks or even months scared, hungry, and tired in order to be free. But for many slaves the hardship and danger were worthwhile after they rode to freedom on the secret rails of the Underground Railroad.

CHAPTER 2

Who Were the Passengers on the Underground Railroad?

Runaway slaves were called "passengers" when they escaped to freedom on the Underground Railroad. But there were no tickets to buy or seats to ride on. These passengers were following a path to the North. They walked through woods, rode on wagons, slept in barns, and hid on boats. Sometimes slaves on the Underground Railroad were also called "packages" or "cargo."

Running Away

Running away was a big decision for slaves.

Running away meant they were leaving their family and friends behind. They were leaving the slave world they knew for a free world they did not know.

FACT

Many slaves ran away at Christmas. They knew their owners would be too busy to notice they were gone.

Slaves running away had to plan their escapes. They could carry only a few belongings. They had to trust people along the way. They had to keep up their courage on the long road to freedom. But the chance for freedom was worth the hardship and danger.

Getting Onboard the Underground Railroad

Most runaway slaves had help from slaves who were not running away. These slaves were the first conductors runaway slaves met on the

Underground Railroad. They shared what little food and clothing they had. They shared their knowledge of the safest routes north. They warned the runaway slaves of dangerous people and places.

In the Free States

Runaway slaves were helped by many African-American and white conductors when they reached the free northern states. These conductors gave their passengers food, clothing, money, and medicine. They helped the runaway slaves find jobs and homes.

But they still were not safe. Due to slave laws, runaway slaves could be captured at any time and returned to their owners.

Canada, Land of the Free

Many slaves rode the Underground Railroad to Canada. Slavery was not allowed in Canada. In Canada, runaway slaves did not have to worry about ever being returned to their owners in the United States.

Thousands of free African Americans lived in Canada. These former slaves owned their own homes. They farmed their own farms. They ran their own businesses. They worshipped in their own churches. And their children went to school for the very first time.

A Great Escape

Ellen and William Craft were married slaves living in Georgia. They knew they had a long, difficult journey to reach freedom in the North. Ellen was very light-skinned. She pretended to be a sick young white man going north to see a famous doctor. Her husband William pretended to be her slave. Together the Crafts rode a real railroad to freedom!

After their daring escape the Crafts worked hard to raise money so other slaves could be free, too.

A Real Underground Railroad "Package"

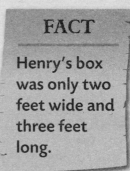
Henry Brown was a slave in Virginia. He decided to ship himself to freedom in a wooden box. A white friend nailed Henry's box shut and shipped him to Philadelphia. Henry rode in trains and wagons for over 24 hours. When Henry's box was opened up, he was a free man! Henry "Box" Brown often spoke about his ride to freedom

to raise money to help other slaves ride the Underground Railroad.

Unknown Passengers

There were thousands of passengers on the Underground Railroad whose daring escapes to freedom will never be known. Many runaway slaves did not share their stories. They did not want people to know their escape routes. They did not want people to know who their conductors were. They did not want people to find out who their owners were.

Today we know only parts of the Underground Railroad story. Much of what happened on the Underground Railroad was secret. We will never know everything about the network of people, places, and pathways of the Underground Railroad. But we do know that thousands of slaves rode the Underground Railroad to freedom.

CHAPTER 3

Who Conducted the Underground Railroad?

There were many African-American and white conductors on the Underground Railroad. Some conductors gave runaway slaves food and safe places to hide. Other conductors took runaway slaves to the next station on the Underground Railroad. Thousands of slaves had these brave conductors to thank for their ride to freedom.

Harriet Tubman

Harriet Tubman is one of the most famous Underground Railroad conductors. Harriet was

Offered for the capture of
Harriet Tubman
~ Fugitive Slave ~

FACT

There was a reward of $40,000 offered for the capture of Harriet Tubman.

a slave in Maryland. After she ran away to freedom in Pennsylvania, Harriet wanted other slaves to be free, too.

Risking her own freedom, Harriet returned to Maryland many times. She wore disguises. She tricked slave owners. Harriet conducted over 300 slaves to freedom! Harriet said proudly, "On my Underground Railroad I never ran my train off the track and I never lost a passenger."

Frederick Douglass

Frederick Douglass was a slave in Maryland. One day he decided to run away. He dressed like a sailor and sailed to freedom on a ship. As a free man, Frederick Douglass began his own newspaper to spread the word against slavery. Douglass called his newspaper *The North Star*, for the star which guided slaves to freedom. Douglass conducted dozens of runaway slaves on the Underground Railroad to freedom in Canada from his station home in Rochester, New York.

Levi and Catherine Coffin

Levi and Catherine Coffin were conductors on the Underground Railroad in Ohio. Their home was an important station. The Coffins gave food, shelter, and clothing to the passengers who stopped at their station. Sometimes, runaway slaves lived for weeks in

the Coffins' home. And no one but the Coffins knew they were there!

The Coffins helped over 2,000 slaves travel north on the Underground Railroad.

William Still

William Still was an important conductor on the Philadelphia route of the Underground Railroad. William Still gave runaway slaves food and money and helped them find jobs. He sent slaves north on the Underground Railroad. He talked with the

The Underground Rail Road

runaway slaves about their lives. When the Underground Railroad stopped running after the Civil War, William Still wrote a book called *The Underground Railroad*. His book told the daring stories of slaves riding to freedom.

John Rankin

John Rankin lived high on Liberty Hill in Ripley, Ohio. Runaway slaves in Kentucky could see John Rankin's house across the Ohio River. The slaves knew John Rankin would help them when they reached his house after crossing the river.

At night, John Rankin hung a lantern in his house. If the lantern was lit, slaves knew it was safe to come to the Rankin house. For forty years John Rankin and his family helped runaway slaves on the Underground Railroad.

FACT

Rankin's thirteen children were conductors, too.

Underground Railroad Conductors

Some Underground Railroad conductors like Harriet Tubman and Frederick Douglass became famous. There were many other conductors who will never be known for helping slaves escape to freedom. But without their secret help many runaway slaves would have missed their rides on the Underground Railroad.

CHAPTER 4

How Did Runaway Slaves Follow the Underground Railroad?

Every runaway slave had to find his or her own road to freedom. Some made it to the North on their own. Thousands more rode the Underground Railroad to freedom in the North or Canada.

A Big Secret

Many people in the North and South knew about the Underground Railroad. But the Underground Railroad routes were kept secret so slave owners could not find their runaway slaves. The Underground Railroad secrets were shared only with people who could be trusted.

Secret Songs and Signs

Secret signals helped the slaves ride the Underground Railroad. Conductors sang songs telling slaves when it was safe to run away or when to hide. Conductors hung lanterns in their windows. A light in the night meant it was safe to move on the Underground Railroad. "A friend with friends" was a secret code telling a conductor that passengers had arrived at his station.

FACT

Birdcalls were used as secret signals.

Codes in Quilts

Quilts with secret messages in them helped slaves escape on the Underground Railroad.

Some quilts were maps showing safe routes north. A Flying Geese pattern on a quilt hanging on a clothesline might have told slaves it was safe to head north. A slave

owner might see the quilt but not know the quilt's secret meaning hidden in plain view.

Freedom Nearby

Slaves in Virginia, Maryland, Delaware, and Kentucky did not have to travel far to be free. These southern states were near free northern states. Slaves were free once they reached Pennsylvania, Ohio, Indiana, and Illinois. The Ohio River flowed 350 miles

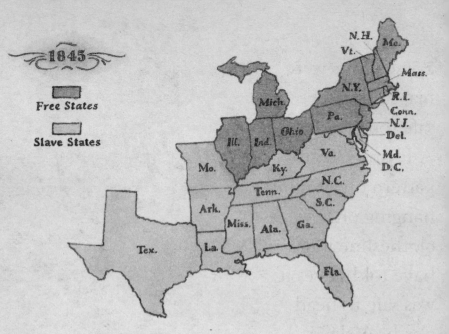

Free States

Slave States

N.H.
Vt.
Mc.
Mass.
N.Y.
R.I.
Mich.
Conn.
Pa.
N.J.
Del.
Ohio
Ill. Ind.
Va.
Md.
D.C.
Mo.
Ky.
N.C.
Tenn.
Ark.
S.C.
Miss. Ala. Ga.
Tex.
La.
Fla.

between slave states and many free states. Runaway slaves were free once they crossed the Ohio River. But there was danger along the way. Laws said runaway slaves could be captured in the free states. Then the slaves were returned in chains to their masters.

A Long, Difficult Road

Slaves running away from Mississippi, Alabama, Florida, Georgia, Louisiana,

Tennessee, and South Carolina had a long way to go to be free. Some hid on steamboats going up the Mississippi River. Others slipped secretly aboard ships sailing north. Most walked hundreds of dangerous miles to freedom. They hid in swamps and forests during the day. They traveled at night. Along the way many conductors helped them on the Underground Railroad.

Springtime

Many slaves ran away in the spring. They followed the geese flying north. Spring rains washed away their footprints and their scents. Slave catchers and their dogs could not follow the runaway slaves' trail.

Slaves often ran away on Saturday nights because Sunday was a day of rest. Running all

FACT

A book called *Uncle Tom's Cabin* was written about the evils of slavery.

night Saturday and Sunday gave the slaves a head start before they would be missed by their owners on Monday morning.

"Follow the Drinking Gourd"

Many slaves knew the song "Follow the Drinking Gourd." This song guided slaves north to freedom. The Drinking Gourd was another name for a group of stars called the Big

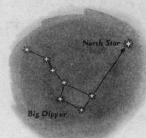

Dipper. The two front stars in the Big Dipper's bowl point to the North Star. When slaves followed the North Star they knew they were going north toward freedom.

"When the sun come back,
When the first quail call,
Then the time is come
Follow the Drinking Gourd."

CHAPTER 5

Were All African-Americans Slaves?

No, not all African-Americans were slaves. During the days of the Underground Railroad, slavery was against the law in the North. Millions of African-Americans were slaves in the South. But some African-Americans lived freely in the North and the South.

Free African-Americans

Free African-Americans living in the northern states had many different jobs. They sailed on ships. They worked on farms. They

FACT

In 1860, there were 500,000 free African-Americans in the North.

lived and worked in cities. Life was not easy for these African-Americans. Often they were not treated fairly. They were not paid as much as white workers. But no one owned them. They were free!

A few free African-Americans lived in the South. Sometimes their owners had let them buy their freedom or released them. Free African-Americans in the South had to be very careful. Sometimes people pretended these African-Americans were not free and sold them back into slavery!

The First Africans in America

In 1619, a ship landed at Jamestown, Virginia. Twenty African men stepped onto America's shores. These men were the first Africans in the English colonies. They had not wanted to come to America. They had been taken away from their families in Africa.

These first African-Americans were servants, not slaves. No one owned them. They worked hard for food to eat and beds to sleep in. They were not paid any money for five years. After that they were free to do what they wanted.

Soon many more Africans were brought to America. But these Africans were not servants. They were captured in Africa to be slaves in America.

The Journey to America

Coming to America was a long, hard trip for the Africans. After being taken from their homes, African men, women, and children were put on slave ships. Each person only had enough space to lie down. They were chained together. They had little to eat and drink.

Many Africans died before reaching

America. The Africans who reached America were then sold to colonists. They were now slaves.

Slave Life Was Hard

Life was hard in the early English colonies. Trees had to be cut down to make farms out of the thick forests. Crops like tobacco, rice, sugar, wheat, and cotton had to be planted

FACT

Sometimes the voyage to America took three months!

and harvested. These products had to be packed and shipped to England.

English colonists could not do all of the work themselves. They needed help, but they didn't want to pay someone to do it for them. So they bought slaves from Africa to do these hard jobs. The slaves cost money to buy, but they worked for free for the rest of their lives.

Slavery in the South

Most southern slaves worked on plantations. Plantations needed many workers. Some plantations had over one hundred slaves! The slaves worked hard in the fields. They cooked, cleaned, and made clothes.

WORD TO KNOW

Plantations **were big farms.**

If a slave owner needed money, he might sell some of his slaves. African-American husbands and wives were often sold to different owners. Children were sold away from their parents.

The Declaration of Independence

The Declaration of Independence said that all people were equal. But southern colonists did not think this meant that African-Americans were their equals.

The United States won its independence from England in 1783. Then many northern states made slavery against the law. After 1808, a law said no more slaves could be brought to the United States from Africa.

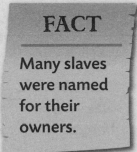

But this did not end slavery in America. African-Americans born in the southern states were still slaves. And many Africans were still captured and brought to America in secret.

Skilled Workers

Many slaves had special skills. Some were blacksmiths, carpenters, sailors, and cooks. Others were good at making cloth and sewing clothes.

Some slaves were sent by their owners to work at other plantations. Sometimes these owners gave their slaves a little of the money they had earned.

Some slaves saved their money to buy their own freedom. If they could, these free African-Americans bought their wives and children. But this did not happen very often, so many brave slaves ran away on the Underground Railroad.

CHAPTER 6

Was the Civil War Fought to End Slavery?

When most people think about the Civil War, they think it was about slavery. They think that the South wanted to keep slavery and the North wanted to stop it. But the Civil War was really fought to keep the United States together as one country. Ending slavery became the purpose of the war only after two long years of fighting.

Before the Civil War

In 1860, Abraham Lincoln was elected President of the United States. People in the northern states were happy about their new president. But people in the southern states were not happy. They worried that President Lincoln would put an end to slavery. Even if they thought slavery was wrong, they needed slaves to work in their fields. But more importantly, they didn't think the country had the right to tell them what to do. They believed that it was up to each state to make its own decisions.

The Confederate States of America

Some of the states in the South decided that they didn't want to be part of the United States anymore. They decided to secede from the United States so they could govern themselves. They started their own country called the Confederate States of America.

> **WORD TO KNOW**
>
> To *secede* means to "break away or to leave."

Soon there were eleven states in the Confederates States of America. They even elected their own president – Jefferson Davis.

President Lincoln Disagrees

President Lincoln believed states could not just leave the United States any time they wanted to. He said the southern states

Confederate Flag

could not be their own country. They were still part of the United States. Abraham Lincoln said he was president of *all* the United States.

> **FACT**
>
> Union was another name for the United States.

No one knew if President Lincoln would go to war to keep the Union together.

The Civil War Begins

President Lincoln did not want a war within his country. He said, "There will be no blood shed unless it be forced upon the Government." He wanted to put the country back together peacefully. But the new Confederate government was willing to fight. They started their own army.

Fort Sumter was a fort on the coast of South Carolina. It was built by the United States government to guard the harbor from enemies. Since it was in the South, the Confederate government thought the fort should belong to them.

On April 12, 1861, southern troops attacked Fort Sumter. After this attack,

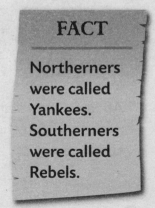

President Lincoln had no choice but to fight back. The Civil War had begun.

A Country at War

No one thought the war would last a long time. When President Lincoln asked men to join the fight, he asked them to volunteer for only three months. But the Civil War went on for four long years. Most of the

> **FACT**
>
> Northerners were called Yankees. Southerners were called Rebels.

fighting took place in the South. Cities were destroyed. Families were torn apart. Thousands of lives were lost.

Freedom

After two years, President Lincoln decided that he had to do something. He promised to free the slaves in the South. If the slaves were free, they wouldn't be there to work on the plantations. This would weaken the Confederacy. Also, the free slaves could join the Union army.

FACT

By the end of the war, 180,000 African-American men served in the Union army.

Lincoln's promise changed the purpose of the Civil War. The war was started to keep the country from splitting into two. Now the war was also being fought to free the slaves.

CHAPTER 7

How Did Abraham Lincoln Use Words to End Slavery?

Abraham Lincoln knew the power of words. He liked to read them, speak them, and write them. Abraham Lincoln used his own powerful words to win the Civil War and end slavery.

Young Abe Sees Slaves

There were slaves in Kentucky when Abraham Lincoln was born there in 1809. When he grew older, Abe's parents told him slavery was wrong.

One day, young Abe saw slaves walking on a road near the Lincoln's cabin. The slaves

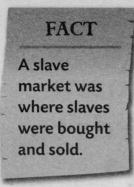

were chained together. Their owner carried a long whip. When Abe was twenty-two years old he visited New Orleans. He saw a slave market for the first time in his life. Abe was upset that humans were being treated like animals. Abe said, "If I ever get a chance to hit that thing (slavery), I'll hit it hard."

A House Divided

While running for president in 1858, Abraham Lincoln made his famous "House Divided" speech.

Abraham Lincoln remembered a Bible story he had read as a boy. The story said that if a house is split in half, it could not stand strong. Abraham Lincoln thought the United

States was like that split house, half slave and half free. He said, "A house divided against itself cannot stand....I believe this government cannot endure . . . half slave and half free."

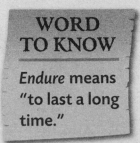

The Emancipation Proclamation

On January 1, 1863, President Abraham Lincoln signed the Emancipation Proclamation, which announced his view on slavery to the whole country.

In the Emancipation Proclamation, President Lincoln wrote, "I do order and declare that all persons held as slaves . . . shall be free."

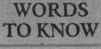

President Lincoln usually signed his name *A. Lincoln*. But he felt the Emancipation Proclamation was so important that he signed *Abraham Lincoln*.

The Gettysburg Address

In July of 1863, the Union Army won an important battle at Gettysburg, Pennsylvania. During that battle thousands of Union and Confederate soldiers died.

WORD TO KNOW

An *address* means "a speech."

On November 19, 1863, President Lincoln gave his famous Gettysburg Address. He spoke at the cemetery where many of the soldiers were buried.

Abraham Lincoln said, "Four score and seven years ago our fathers brought forth on this continent, a new nation, conceived in Liberty, and dedicated to the proposition that all men are created equal."

President Lincoln's speech was only 268 words long. But his powerful words made people understand that all Americans, whether white or African-American, were equal.

FACT

A *score* is 20 years, so four score and seven years is 87 years. The Declaration of Independence had been signed 87 years earlier.

The End of Slavery

In 1864, President Lincoln wrote, "I am naturally anti-slavery. If slavery is not wrong, nothing is wrong. I can not remember when I did not think so."

On January 31, 1865, just before the Civil War ended, Congress made slavery against the law everywhere in the United States forever. Slavery had finally ended. Abraham Lincoln's powerful words had helped.

President Lincoln's Dreams

President Lincoln did not live long enough to enjoy his success. On April 15, 1865, President Abraham Lincoln died after being shot by John Wilkes Booth.

But Abraham Lincoln's powerful words had helped his dreams come true. All of the United States were united again and slavery had ended.